Original title:
Laughter's Glow in the Night Sky

Copyright © 2025 Swan Charm
All rights reserved.

Author: Aron Pilviste
ISBN HARDBACK: 978-9908-1-3544-1
ISBN PAPERBACK: 978-9908-1-3545-8
ISBN EBOOK: 978-9908-1-3546-5

A Tapestry of Smiles in the Darkness

In shadows deep we weave our thread,
A tapestry of joy where fears are shed.
With laughter bright against the gloom,
Each smile a flower, brightening the room.

Through whispered laughs, the night's embrace,
We dance beneath the moon's soft grace.
In echoes of delight, we find our peace,
Transforming every frown, the sorrow will cease.

Pixelated Joy on the Infinite Canvas

In pixels small, our dreams collide,
A canvas vast, where colors reside.
Each joyful spark ignites the night,
As laughter dances in the light.

A brush of love on a digital skin,
Where every heartbeat echoes within.
We craft our stories, vivid and bright,
Painting the world with pure delight.

Nocturnal Fun in the Starlit Grove

Underneath the stars, we roam so free,
In a secret grove, just you and me.
The night air hums with laughter and cheer,
Our joy resounding, crystal clear.

With fireflies dancing, we share our dreams,
In whispered tales, nothing's as it seems.
The moon our witness, shining above,
In the starlit grove, we find our love.

Ethereal Larks Beneath the Night

In twilight's grasp, our voices soar,
Ethereal larks that light the shore.
With every note, the darkness fades,
In harmony, a serenade.

Beneath the stars, our spirits play,
In magic whispers, night turns to day.
With laughter flowing, like a gentle stream,
We weave our hopes into a dream.

The Playful Dance of the Celestials

Stars twirl in a cosmic flight,
Winking softly in the night.
Planets spin with joyous glee,
Caught in the dance of destiny.

Galaxies swirl, a flowing stream,
Whispers echo like a dream.
Comets race with tails of light,
Painting wonders in the night.

Nebulas bloom in colors bright,
A canvas born from celestial sight.
Asteroids glide on paths unknown,
Carving tales in the cosmic zone.

Moonbeams pirouette through the air,
Gentle breezes everywhere.
Cosmic rhythms guide their way,
In this dance where starlight plays.

Caught in wonder, we all gaze,
Enchanted by the eternal maze.
The universe sings sweet and clear,
In the dance that we hold dear.

Illuminated Dreams in the Ether

Soft whispers float through twilight air,
Dreams illuminated, free from care.
In the ether, thoughts take flight,
Painting visions in the night.

Silver threads of starlit grace,
Weave through time and endless space.
Imaginations brightly gleam,
As we chase our waking dream.

Clouds shimmer with a silken hue,
Reflecting hopes both old and new.
In this realm where shadows play,
We find our fears begin to sway.

Echoes of laughter fill the sky,
In the dance where dreams can fly.
Hearts uplifted, spirits free,
In the glow of infinity.

As the dawn begins to break,
We hold close the dreams we make.
Illuminated by the light,
In this world of endless night.

Brightness Amongst Darkened Skies

Amidst the gloom, a beacon glows,
Whispers of light where hope bestows.
Stars emerge like diamonds rare,
Illuminating the velvet air.

Shadows fade as dawn draws near,
Bringing colors, vibrant and clear.
A symphony of warmth unfolds,
In the embrace of sunlit golds.

Moonlight dances on the lake,
Crafting beauty that we partake.
Reflections shimmer, soft and bright,
Guiding hearts through endless night.

Every spark ignites a dream,
In the darkness, love's warm beam.
Together we rise, hand in hand,
Finding brightness in the land.

With each heartbeat, we transcend,
In this journey without end.
Amongst the dark, we see the skies,
Filled with dreams and sweet goodbyes.

Harmonies of Joy in the Nocturne

The night unfurls its velvet cloak,
In each corner, soft echoes evoke.
Luna sings her gentle song,
In the heart where dreams belong.

Crickets play their midnight tune,
Composing symphonies with the moon.
Each note dances on the breeze,
Melodies float through ancient trees.

Stars harmonize in the deep blue,
Creating music, ever true.
In the silence, joy takes flight,
Painting visions in the night.

The world breathes slow, a quiet sigh,
Underneath the expansive sky.
In this nocturne, we belong,
In the rhythm of love's sweet song.

Hand in hand, we drift away,
Where the night leads hearts to play.
In the harmony, we find peace,
In the nocturne, our souls release.

Gleeful Murmurs Beneath the Firmament

Stars twinkle bright, dancing on high,
Whispers of joy float through the sky.
Laughter echoes, a sweet refrain,
In the night's warmth, we feel no pain.

Moonlight bathes the world in gold,
Stories of wonder, forever told.
Hearts entwined in celestial glow,
Under the cosmos, dreams freely flow.

Shooting stars, a magical sight,
We make our wishes into the night.
Silent secrets shared with the breeze,
In this realm, our souls find ease.

Gleeful murmurs rise from below,
As the night sky puts on a show.
We dance in shadows, our spirits soar,
Beneath the firmament, we want no more.

Celestial Comforts of Mirth

In the soft hush of twilight's hue,
Celestial comforts whisper to you.
Mirthful sighs ride on the breeze,
Moments flutter, like dancing leaves.

Stars gather close, a glittering crew,
Painting the heavens in shades of blue.
Each twinkling light, a joyous spark,
Guiding our hearts through the gentle dark.

With each heartbeat, a laughter swells,
In soft embrace, the silence dwells.
Time pauses, as we bask in grace,
In this sanctuary, we find our place.

The moon smiles down, a knowing friend,
Wrapping us tight, as dreams ascend.
In celestial comfort, fears take flight,
We dance in the shadows, embracing the night.

Twilight Revels of the Heart

As daylight fades and colors blend,
Twilight calls, an enchanting friend.
Hearts awaken with a gentle beat,
Revels of joy where shadows meet.

The horizon blushes, a fiery kiss,
In this moment, we find pure bliss.
Laughter mingles with the evening's sigh,
Under the stars, we dare to fly.

Whispers of love float on the air,
In twilight's embrace, free from care.
Every glance shared is a promise made,
In the dance of dusk, no fears invade.

We twirl in the soft, fading light,
Painting our dreams in colors so bright.
Twilight revels, a symphony sweet,
At the heart of the night, every pulse, every beat.

Dreamy Whimsies in the Night's Embrace

In the stillness where shadows play,
Dreamy whimsies drift and sway.
Soft serenades of the night's song,
Urging the weary to dance along.

Beneath the whispers of the starlit sky,
Imagination takes wing to fly.
Every heartbeat, a tale unfolds,
In the night's embrace, adventure calls.

Velvet dreams wrap us in delight,
As we chase the moon's soft light.
A tapestry woven with softest thread,
In the night's embrace, our spirits wed.

In clouds of wonder, we gently drift,
Each moment shared, a precious gift.
In the realm of dreams, where silence breathes,
We dance through the night, as magic weaves.

Whispers of Joy in the Twilight

In the hush of dusk, whispers roam,
Lingering sweet, like a soft poem.
Colors dance in the fading light,
Hearts ignite in the gentle night.

Laughter flutters on the breeze,
Carrying secrets through the trees.
Each sound a treasure, softly spun,
Echoing stories of days gone by.

Golden hues melt into gray,
As joy wraps dusk in sweet ballet.
Promises linger as shadows blend,
Whispers of joy that never end.

Stars awaken, gleaming bright,
Stirring dreams in the still of night.
Every moment, a chance to share,
Whispers of joy float in the air.

Radiant Chuckles Under Starlit Veils

Beneath the canvas of night's embrace,
Laughter twinkles, a radiant trace.
In every chuckle, a star is born,
Lighting the dark until the dawn.

Silent giggles drift through the air,
Wrapped in starlight, light as a prayer.
Each chuckle a spark, a joyful feat,
Dancing softly, like hearts that beat.

Golden laughter spreads like fire,
Igniting dreams, lifting them higher.
With every burst, shadows recede,
Radiant chuckles plant joyful seed.

The moon smiles down, a witness near,
To all the laughter we've held dear.
In starlit veils, memories play,
Radiant chuckles, life's grand ballet.

Serenade of Glee Beneath the Moon

Beneath the moon's soft, silver glow,
A serenade of joy begins to flow.
Each note a whisper, sweet and clear,
Drawing loved ones close, holding them near.

Melodies twirl like leaves in flight,
Filling the world with sheer delight.
In the cool embrace of the night air,
Glee finds roots, growing everywhere.

Stars listen closely as dreams take wing,
Echoing laughter, the heart's own sing.
Every harmony, a moment shared,
In this serenade, we are paired.

Softly the shadows sway and dance,
Caught in the rhythm, lost in the trance.
A serenade played just for two,
Beneath the moon, love feels anew.

Celestial Giggles in the Dark

In the silence where dreams reside,
Celestial giggles cannot hide.
They sparkle softly in the night,
Whispering joy, a pure delight.

As stars twinkle, laughter weaves,
Through the branches, the world believes.
Each giggle a star, shining bright,
Lighting up shadows, banishing fright.

In the darkness, hope takes flight,
With celestial giggles, pure and right.
A melody carried on the breeze,
Caressing hearts with gentle ease.

Every sigh accompanies a laugh,
Moments cherished, a curious craft.
In silence, they weave a cosmic song,
Celestial giggles where we belong.

Luminescent Heartbeats in the Dark

In shadows deep, where whispers roam,
The heart ignites, a fiery home.
Soft pulses glow, a tender spark,
Illuminating paths through dark.

Each breath a dance, a rhythm sweet,
In silence, melodies softly meet.
The stars above, they weave and thread,
In this embrace, no words are said.

With every thump, a tale unfolds,
In quiet night, the story molds.
A luminescent glow in the haze,
Awakens dreams in frosty bays.

In deepened breaths, the night ignites,
A symphony of soft delights.
With heartbeats pure, we light the way,
Through darkest nights into the day.

A tender touch, like embers warm,
In hidden realms where spirits swarm.
With every beat, a world reborn,
In darkness, whispers softly adorn.

And when the dawn begins to break,
These heartbeats sing, a life awake.
For love is light that leads us through,
In luminescent shades of you.

The Cosmic Carnival After Dusk

Beneath the stars, where dreams collide,
A carnival unfurls its pride.
With whispers sweet in evening air,
The cosmic show begins to share.

Bright colors dance, in shadows leap,
As laughter spills and secrets keep.
The galaxies spin, a merry-go-round,
In stellar joy, lost souls are found.

A ticket glimmers, just for one,
To ride the waves of moonlit fun.
With every turn, a wish takes flight,
In cosmic realms, where hearts ignite.

The merry tunes of time and space,
Invite us all to join the chase.
With joyful hearts, we explore the night,
In this vast dance, we find our light.

Unfurling dreams like paper sails,
Through cosmic storms and gentle gales.
Each heartbeat sings, a vibrant call,
In this grand show, we find it all.

When dusk surrenders to morning's glow,
The carnival fades, but memories flow.
In starry nights, we'll replay the art,
Of the cosmic carnival within our heart.

Mirthful Glimmers Through the Abyss

In depths unseen, where shadows creep,
A glimmer stirs from ancient sleep.
Soft laughter swells in murky tides,
As joy escapes where darkness hides.

The abyss may echo with silent fears,
But mirthful glimmers dry our tears.
With every spark, the void ignites,
In laughter's warmth, the coldness fights.

Dancing echoes weave through the night,
Reminding souls of hidden light.
For in the shadows, colors bloom,
A vibrant dance dispels the gloom.

With every step, we break the chains,
In joy, we find what still remains.
To twirl and laugh amidst the vast,
As echoes of our hearts contrast.

Through thickened air, a radiance flows,
Transforming fears to wondrous shows.
In glorious bursts, through darkness roam,
These mirthful glimmers call us home.

And when the dawn paints skies anew,
The abyss bows low, as light breaks through.
With joyful hearts, we've paved the way,
For mirthful glimmers guide our stay.

Whimsy and Wonder Under the Canopy

In forest depths, where secrets play,
The trees whisper in soft ballet.
With starlit leaves, they weave a spell,
Of whimsy and wonder, all is well.

The moonlight dances on petals fair,
With gentle glows, it fills the air.
In shadows deep, the fairies twirl,
Awakening dreams in every whirl.

Each rustling branch tells tales anew,
Of magic lost and friendships true.
With every step on mossy ground,
A world of wonder can be found.

Through hidden paths where wild things roam,
We find our hearts gently call it home.
In every twist, a story flows,
Of whimsy's essence, as nature glows.

When morning comes, the canopy sings,
Of joyful days and simple things.
With laughter bright, we share our cheer,
In this wild place where kinships steer.

And as the sun dips low in sight,
The canopy glows with warmth and light.
For whimsy and wonder forever stay,
In nature's harmony, come what may.

Mischief Among Celestial Bodies

In the night, the stars conspire,
Whispers of laughter, sparks of fire.
Jupiter winks, a playful tease,
While Saturn sways in cosmic breeze.

Comets dash with a dazzling flight,
Playing hide and seek through the night.
Galaxies twirl in a waltz of light,
Fleeting shadows, a wondrous sight.

Nebulas chuckle, a curtain drawn,
Dancing in silence until the dawn.
Cosmic mischief fills the air,
Each twinkle a tale, a secret shared.

Stardust Serenades of Happiness

In the cradle of night, whispers sing,
Melodies soft as a star's gentle wing.
Stardust drips from the skies above,
Weaving a tapestry spun from love.

Cascades of joy in the moon's embrace,
Every note finds its perfect place.
Hearts dance lightly on beams of light,
Basking in warmth, the world feels right.

Galactic harmonies swell and soar,
Echoes of laughter that beckon for more.
Each twinkle a promise, a wish on the breeze,
In stardust serenades, find your peace.

Bubbles of Joy in the Moonlight

In moonlit pools, bubbles arise,
Reflecting dreams in the starlit skies.
Each pop a giggle, each rise a cheer,
Joy dances lightly, free from fear.

Floating softly, the night holds tight,
Bubbles of joy in the silver light.
A gentle breeze carries laughter near,
Echoing wishes for all to hear.

With every burst, hopes take flight,
Sparking adventures in the night.
In shadows and light, together they play,
Bubbles of joy, sweet moments to stay.

Ethereal Chuckles Amidst the Stars

Under the wonder of the vast night sky,
Ethereal chuckles drift softly by.
Sirius and Vega share secret jokes,
While Orion winks at playful folks.

Constellations giggle, a symphony bright,
Twinkling softly, they dance in delight.
The universe hums a tune serene,
In laughter's embrace, all spaces between.

Galactic whispers, a joyful refrain,
Echoing softly, a celestial chain.
Amidst the stars, where dreams convene,
Ethereal chuckles keep laughter evergreen.

Echoes of Joy from Cosmic Shores

Waves of laughter crash and play,
Stars are dancing, skies so gay.
In the night, the spirits soar,
Joyful whispers on the shore.

Footprints imprinted in the sand,
Fleeting moments, hand in hand.
Echoes call from far and wide,
Hearts align, the universeide.

Moonlit paths guide our delight,
Every heartbeat shines so bright.
Songs of joy, a cosmic tune,
Woven under the silver moon.

With each wave, the laughter swells,
In the air, the magic dwells.
From the deep, our spirits rise,
Bathed in love, under the skies.

In the twilight, memories weave,
Tender moments, we believe.
As stars twinkle, our hopes align,
Echoes of joy, eternally shine.

The Glitter of Cheer in Dusk's Arms

Softly falls the evening light,
Dusk embraces, holding tight.
Glimmering stars begin to twinkle,
In their glow, our hearts do sprinkle.

Laughter dances in the breeze,
Whispered secrets through the trees.
Joyful echoes, sweet and clear,
In this haven, there's no fear.

Colors fade to shades of gold,
Cherished tales of love retold.
On the canvas of the night,
Glittering dreams take flight.

With each moment, joy is found,
In the heart, a vibrant sound.
Dusk unfolds her gentle charm,
Wrapped in cheer, safe from harm.

Together, we chase the light,
As the stars ignite the night.
In this bliss, we find our way,
The glitter of cheer holds sway.

Cosmic Kisses and Giddy Whispers

In the vastness, time stands still,
Galaxies spin, our hearts will thrill.
Cosmic kisses, soft and bold,
In the embrace, stories unfold.

Giddy whispers in the air,
Magic moments, beyond compare.
Stars collide in playful dance,
In their light, we take a chance.

Each touch feels like a sweet surprise,
Filling our souls, blissful ties.
In this realm, we find our peace,
Through cosmic dreams, our joys increase.

Laughter echoes through the night,
Guided by love's gentle light.
In the silence, hearts connect,
Cosmic truths that we protect.

With each breath, the universe sways,
In this love, our spirits blaze.
Giddy whispers, endless flight,
Kisses shared in the starry night.

Celestial Revelations of Humor

Heavens sparkle with laughter bright,
Joys unfold in the soft twilight.
Cosmic humor weaves its thread,
In the mind, its joy is spread.

Twinkling stars, a playful jest,
In these moments, we are blessed.
Celestial sparks ignite the air,
Laughter lingers everywhere.

With each quip, the universe grins,
In our hearts, deep joy begins.
Humor flows like a gentle stream,
A cosmic bond, a shared dream.

Jests from stars above the earth,
Remind us all of life's true worth.
In the light, our spirits rise,
Celestial joy beneath the skies.

So let us laugh, let voices sing,
Open hearts to what joy can bring.
In this dance, we find our play,
Humor guides us on our way.

Cosmic Laughter Weaving Through the Night

Stars blink gently, winking bright,
Whispers of joy dance in flight.
Galaxies twirl in joyous glee,
Echoes of laughter, wild and free.

Moonlight spills on dreams so bold,
Stories of love, secretly told.
Cosmic winds carry joyful tunes,
As night blooms under silver moons.

A tapestry spun of radiant light,
Each sparkle sings of pure delight.
In the vastness, hearts intertwine,
Under the stars, our souls align.

Twinkling gems in velvet space,
Every heartbeat finds its place.
We are stardust, woven tight,
In the arms of the cosmic night.

With laughter echoing through the dark,
We paint the sky with our spark.
Together we dance, spirits high,
Cosmic laughter, never shy.

Playful Stardust Amidst the Astral Glow

In the stillness, stardust plays,
Whirling in the Milky Way's haze.
Winks and giggles dazzle bright,
Playful spirits take to flight.

Comets streak with laughter loud,
Floating freely, never bowed.
Nebulae share their secrets old,
Encapsulated in hues of gold.

Celestial whispers spark our dreams,
Painted light in silvery beams.
Each twinkle tells a tale of bliss,
In this vast unknown abyss.

Echoing through the endless skies,
A cosmic joie de vivre that flies.
With every heartbeat, we unite,
In the dance of stardust light.

Embers of joy, softly aglow,
Floating on winds of astral flow.
Together, we spin in joy and cheer,
In the universe, forever near.

The Twilight Canvas of Joveness

In twilight's arms, we find our bliss,
Moments captured in a gentle kiss.
Fading light paints vibrant hues,
A canvas rich with evening's muse.

Youthful laughter lingers sweet,
As day and night converge, we meet.
The horizon blooms in fiery glow,
Where dreams awaken, row by row.

Stars emerge, blush with glee,
Whispers of youth, wild and free.
Each heartbeat echoes tales of grace,
In twilight's warm and tender embrace.

Together we sketch our fate,
Moments fleeting but never late.
With each stroke upon the sky,
A masterpiece that will not die.

In the twilight, we become one,
As shadows dance and day is done.
A tapestry woven with spark and cheer,
In the canvas of joveness, we revere.

Night's Radiance of Joyful Echoes

In the hush of night, echoes ring,
Whispered secrets, joys they bring.
Radiant hues, moonlight's glow,
Crafting dreams that softly flow.

Each echo resonates within,
A symphony where tales begin.
Stars applaud in twinkling cheer,
As we drift through moments dear.

The cosmos hums a gentle tune,
Under the gaze of the watchful moon.
Laughter dances on silken air,
Joyful echoes everywhere.

We sail through night's endless sea,
Breathless with ecstatic glee.
In the stillness, we find our place,
In the night's radiant embrace.

Together we weave through cosmic dreams,
As joyful echoes burst at the seams.
With hearts unbound, forever bright,
In the radiance of the night.

Radiance of Rapture in the Cosmos

In the depth of night, stars ignite,
A celestial dance, pure delight.
Nebulas swirl, colors collide,
Whispers of love in the cosmic tide.

Galaxies turn with graceful art,
Each twinkle a beat, a cosmic heart.
Planets embrace in orbits divine,
Their harmonies weave in space's design.

Comets trail with radiant grace,
Racing through the velvet space.
Lunar beams kissing the ground,
In each soft glow, magic is found.

Shooting stars cross in a flash,
Moments of wonder, dreams to clash.
In the silence, our hearts transcend,
In the rapture, we find our blend.

Cosmic radiance, eternal flight,
Guiding our souls through the night.
Together we soar, wild and free,
In the vastness of eternity.

Cosmic Delights in Shadows

In the void where silence dwells,
A tapestry of secrets tells.
Constellations craft stories bold,
In the dark, their secrets unfold.

Galactic whispers drift and sway,
Through the cosmos, night and day.
Shadows dance with starlit grace,
In hidden realms, we find our place.

Planets murmur soft like dreams,
In cosmic lullabies, it seems.
Auroras flicker, colors blend,
Painting the skies where shadows bend.

A journey unfolds in the dark,
Each shadow flickers, igniting a spark.
With every glimpse, a new delight,
In cosmic shadows, we ignite.

So let us wander, hand in hand,
Through celestial seas of shimmering sand.
In the cosmic night, love takes flight,
Guiding us home with pure delight.

Starry-Eyed Smiles in the Abyss

In the depths where darkness lies,
Starry-eyed dreams begin to rise.
With a smile, hope lights the way,
In the abyss, we choose to stay.

Galaxies swirl with joy and grace,
Each twinkle shares a warm embrace.
Laughter echoes through the night,
In the shadows, we find our light.

Abyssal depths, both vast and wide,
Within the darkness, love won't hide.
With every star, a wish is cast,
In our hearts, the shadows pass.

Dance with me through cosmic gleams,
In the abyss, we'll weave our dreams.
Hand in hand, we'll take the leap,
Creating memories we will keep.

In starry skies, our spirits soar,
As the universe opens its door.
Together we shine, endless and true,
In the abyss, it's me and you.

Enchanted Whispers of the Night

In the stillness of twilight's charm,
Moonlit secrets keep us warm.
Enchanted whispers dance like fire,
Igniting dreams and pure desire.

Stars above weave tales so rare,
Guiding lost souls with tender care.
Celestial breezes softly play,
In whispered hues, they light our way.

Night blooms with a fragrant grace,
In its arms, we find our place.
Through the magic of every sound,
Our hearts in rhythm, love unbound.

As shadows fall and dreams take flight,
We find our solace in the night.
With every heartbeat, whispers grow,
In enchanted realms, love's beauty glows.

Let us wander where starlight beams,
In the night, we'll weave our dreams.
Together we'll dance on moonlit streets,
In enchanted whispers, our love repeats.

Revelry Among the Stars

In the tapestry of night, they dance,
Whispers of joy in a twinkling glance.
Galaxies spin in a cosmic waltz,
Echoes of laughter, the universe vaults.

From Mars to Venus, they play and glide,
Celestial beings, in jubilation, reside.
Each comet streaks like a firefly's flight,
Revelry blooms in the soft, silver light.

Shooting stars carry wishes and dreams,
Celestial parties, or so it seems.
Melodies linger on the warm night air,
As stardust celebrates without a care.

In the realm of planets, they raise a cheer,
Cosmic champagne, for all who are near.
Together they twirl, with spirits so bright,
A festival woven in the fabric of night.

Time stands still in this wondrous embrace,
With stars as their guides in this magical space.
Infinity sings in this joyful display,
As revelry shines in a luminous way.

Midnight Merriment in the Cosmos

Under the moonlight, shadows play,
In whispers of silver, they find their way.
Galaxies twinkle, a brilliant glow,
Midnight merriment begins to flow.

Planets spin like delicate tops,
In cosmic tunes, their joy never stops.
Nebulas swirl in a colorful dance,
All of the cosmos, lost in a trance.

Shooting stars streak through the velvet sky,
Carrying dreams as they dance and fly.
Echoes of music from stars far away,
Join in the revelry's sweet ballet.

With meteors weaving a shimmering thread,
In the heart of the night where no fears tread.
Laughter erupts like the fireworks' spark,
In the cosmic embrace, they leave their mark.

Floating on beams of the night's gentle grace,
In this boundless realm, they find their place.
Forever together, in starlit delight,
Their midnight merriment glows ever bright.

Joyful Echoes in the Nocturnal Breeze

In the hush of the evening, secrets unfold,
Whispers of joy in the dark, gently told.
Breezes carrying laughter, soft as the night,
Echoes of wonder, in pure delight.

Fragrant blooms sway under the moon,
Nature's soft chorus sings a sweet tune.
In every rustle, a story does weave,
Joyful echoes that never deceive.

Stars peek through leaves, a glittering show,
Guiding the hearts that are ready to grow.
In the stillness, every heartbeat aligns,
With the beauty of night that forever shines.

The world is aglow with a magical light,
As shadows dance under the soft starlight.
Mirth fills the air, a delicate tease,
Carried along in the nocturnal breeze.

With every moment, the night does unfold,
Embracing the warmth of the stories retold.
Each breath a whisper, each sigh a release,
In joyous echoes, we find our peace.

Elysian Rays of Delight

Golden beams pierce through the twilight glow,
Elysian rays whisper, "Come, let us go."
In the embrace of warmth, spirits ignite,
Dancing on clouds in the soft, fading light.

With laughter cascading like rain from the skies,
Breaking the silence, a sweet surprise.
Each ray of sun, a gentle caress,
Filling the world with a radiant dress.

From valleys to mountains, the colors blend,
Creating a canvas that never will end.
Joyfully spiraling, hearts take their flight,
In elysian realms, everything feels right.

Every moment converges in blissful refrain,
Time becomes fluid, a soft, soothing grain.
With hearts intertwined in a luminous night,
We bask in the glory of pure delight.

In the twilight's embrace, dreams take their flight,
As elysian rays weave day into night.
Together we linger, lost in the light,
Forever enchanted, our spirits take flight.

Joyful Twinklings in the Abyss

In the dark where wonders play,
Bright little sparks light the way.
Whispers of dreams, soft and clear,
Dancing with joy, erasing fear.

A symphony of twinkling light,
Guiding the hearts through the night.
Each shimmer tells a tale anew,
Of hope and love, so pure and true.

Beneath the vast and starry dome,
We find our minds a place called home.
In the stillness, laughter rings,
A gentle echo that joy brings.

Every glint, a wish set free,
Floating on waves of mystery.
Joyful twinklings softly sway,
A chorus of night, night and day.

In this abyss, we laugh and sing,
Holding on to the joy they bring.
Forever cherished, these bright lights,
Guide us through the endless nights.

Engulfed in Merriment's Veil

Wrapped in laughter, soft as air,
Merriment fills the light with care.
In every glance, a spark ignites,
Weaving magic through our nights.

The world around us gleams with flair,
Eager hearts beyond compare.
With open arms, we embrace the day,
In merriment's warm and bright array.

Dreams take flight on joyous wings,
In every moment, the joy it brings.
Laughter dances, a vibrant song,
Uniting souls where we belong.

In every corner, joy we find,
A gentle pulse that warms the mind.
Engulfed in mirth, we twirl and spin,
Together as one, let the fun begin.

In the tapestry of time's sweet flow,
Our laughter echoes, soft and low.
Engulfed in merriment's endless sail,
We ride the joy, we shall not fail.

Reflections of Mirth in the Silver Sky

Beneath the sky, so vast and bright,
Reflections dance in morning light.
Mirth abounds in every hue,
Painting the world in smiles anew.

Clouds like cotton drift and sway,
Whispering secrets of the day.
In every shimmer, laughter soars,
Opening wide the joyful doors.

With every breeze, a giggle spun,
Echoing laughter, we become one.
In the warmth of the sun's embrace,
We find our hearts, our own safe space.

The silver sky, a canvas wide,
Holds our dreams, our joys inside.
Reflections of mirth, pure and bright,
Guide us home through the starry night.

In unity, we share this grace,
A fleeting moment, a cherished place.
In the silver sky, our spirits fly,
Forever bound, you and I.

Stars Winking in Delightful Harmony

Above the world, the stars align,
Winking down like jewels divine.
In a dance of light and song,
They guide our hearts where we belong.

Each twinkle tells a secret true,
Of dreams fulfilled and skies so blue.
In delightful harmony they sway,
Leading us through the twilight gray.

A tapestry of joy up high,
Whispers softly, like a sigh.
Beneath this celestial display,
We find our peace, night turns to day.

With every gleam, a story shared,
In unity, we find we dared.
Stars winking as we laugh and play,
In the embrace of night's soft ballet.

Underneath this cosmic dome,
We journey far, but feel at home.
Stars of wonder, shining bright,
Guide our souls into the night.

Flickers of Grin Under the Silent Watch

In twilight's hush, the stars peek out,
Silent whispers, the night's gentle shout.
Flickers of joy in a world so still,
Moments captured, time begins to thrill.

Shadows dance with a flickering light,
Dreams take flight on a soft, starry night.
Under the moon's gaze, hearts intertwine,
In this serene space, everything's fine.

Laughter echoes in the twilight's folds,
Stories shared, as each moment unfolds.
Underneath watchful eyes, joy takes flight,
In the twilight hush, hearts feel so light.

Each flicker brightens the canvas of time,
Painting the night with rhythm and rhyme.
Hope and warmth in the air softly blend,
Under the moon's watch, where dreams never end.

Tranquil hearts find a peaceful embrace,
In flickers of grin, we all find our place.
Through every laugh, in silence we trust,
In the night's tapestry, love is a must.

Lunar Lullabies of Cheerfulness

Moonlight weaves through the evening air,
A lullaby sung without a care.
Gentle breezes sway the trees around,
In lunar glow, pure joy is found.

Soft whispers dance on the silver beams,
Carrying forth the sweetest dreams.
Each star a note in the lullaby,
Echoing softly as night drifts by.

With every heartbeat, laughter is near,
In the glow of night, sadness disappears.
Lunar lullabies, they cradle the soul,
In this warm embrace, we feel whole.

Swaying shadows under the moon's light,
Inviting hearts to join in the flight.
Singing together beneath the vast sky,
In lunar hymns, our spirits comply.

As dawn approaches, the notes begin to fade,
Yet in our hearts, the melody's laid.
Lunar lullabies of cheerfulness stay,
Whispering hope as night turns to day.

Tranquil Whispers and Wondrous Laughter

In quiet corners where echoes play,
Whispers of peace lead the heart away.
Laughter lingers in the gentle air,
Moments of joy floating everywhere.

Sunlight drapes on the budding leaves,
Creating magic that softly weaves.
Each tranquil whisper sings from the heart,
A wondrous melody, a beautiful start.

Together we share in this sacred space,
Laughter and whispers, a loving embrace.
Nature's chorus invites us to hear,
The gentle songs that bring us near.

Through fields of dreams, our spirits soar,
Each tranquil moment holds so much more.
With wondrous laughter painting the sky,
Together we'll dance, forever nearby.

Wrapped in the arms of the evening tide,
Tranquil whispers guide us, our joy open wide.
In laughter and peace, our hearts take flight,
Two souls entwined under the soft moonlight.

Sojourns of Glee Across Celestial Seas

Across the skies where the stars ignite,
Sojourns of glee take joyful flight.
In boats of laughter, we sail and glide,
Over celestial seas, with love as our guide.

Waves of wonder lap at our dreams,
Underneath the starlight, everything gleams.
With hearts unbound, we explore the night,
In sojourns of glee, everything feels right.

Cascading laughter spills like the tide,
Carrying secrets and joy inside.
Every heartbeat echoes, vibrant and free,
Guided by stars across cosmic sea.

As we drift on, the world feels at peace,
In sojourns of glee, troubles never cease.
With every wave and every twinkling star,
We find home in laughter, no matter how far.

Through celestial paths, our spirits will play,
Sojourns of glee, forever they'll stay.
Amongst the galaxies, wild and bright,
Together we journey through day and night.

The Humor Beneath a Velvet Canopy

Under stars that wink and gleam,
Laughter dances in moonlight's dream.
Whispers of joking shadows play,
As night nudges the worries away.

Beneath the canopy of the night,
Joy blooms softly, a radiant sight.
A jester's hat lost in the grass,
Reveals the silliness that will not pass.

Moonbeams sprinkle light like confetti,
While secrets spark, oh so heady.
A smile carved on the face of time,
Echoes in jingles, a cheerful rhyme.

The owls chuckle in their hoots,
As frogs serenade with silly flutes.
Every rustle tells a punchline,
Under the velvet, life is divine.

In the shadows, joy comes to reside,
Where humor and magic collide.
The night, a canvas for laughter's spree,
Under the sky, wild and free.

Celestial Shenanigans at Dusk

As daylight bows to dusk's embrace,
Stars prepare for their velvet race.
Comets giggle, leap and twirl,
In the cosmic dance, they whirl.

Galaxies toss and spin in glee,
In this vast expanse, so carefree.
Moons play hide and seek with light,
Their laughter echoing through the night.

The sun winks down, bidding ado,
While planets gather in bright hues.
Shadows stretch with a playful grin,
As the nighttime revelry begins.

Twinkling stardust coats the sky,
In a playful chaos, spirits fly.
Eclipses tease with a mischievous tune,
Crafting shenanigans, bright as the moon.

Each star a spark in the cosmic jest,
In this theater, we are all guests.
At dusk's curtain-call, we take part,
In the universe's merry heart.

Ethereal Revelry in the Firmament

Beneath the vast, celestial dome,
Ethereal whispers invite us home.
With each twinkling, secrets unfurl,
A celebration in a cosmic whirl.

Shooting stars share tales of delight,
In laughter, they shimmer through the night.
Planets adorn themselves in jest,
In this firmament, we are blessed.

Clouds weave stories in silver lace,
With whimsical wonders, they interlace.
A chorus of comets sing in spree,
As the universe laughs in harmony.

The moon dons a smile, soft and bright,
Guiding us through the velvet night.
With every breath, the cosmos hums,
In ethereal revelry, joy becomes.

Celestial beings twirl in delight,
As the stars sprinkle love, pure and light.
In this heavenly dance, we twine,
Ethereal revelry, a gift divine.

Dreams Stitched with Threads of Merriment

In a tapestry woven with golden dreams,
Stitched with laughter, hope brightly beams.
Every thread, a story to share,
Merriment dances in the air.

Soft whispers of joy crisscross the night,
In each moment, a spark of delight.
Dreams play hide and seek in disguise,
While giggles flutter and rise.

A loom of starlight, detailed and grand,
Weaves our wishes with a gentle hand.
In this fabric, life we design,
Stitched with love, forever entwined.

With every stitch, we weave our fate,
Merriment beckons, never too late.
In the quiet fabric, hearts do conspire,
Dreams stitched together, a soul's desire.

In the quilt of night, friendships grow,
Bound by laughter, a radiant glow.
With threads of joy, the dreamers sing,
In this world, we're free to bring.

Gossamer Threads of Joy in the Night

In the quiet, stars do gleam,
Whispers dance on silver beams.
Laughter echoes through the dark,
Holding warmth like summer's spark.

Crickets sing their lullabies,
Moonlight twinkles in our eyes.
Hearts entwined with soft delight,
Gossamer threads weaving the night.

In the shadows, dreams take flight,
Each moment feels just right.
A canvas painted with our cheer,
Joy's embrace is always near.

Like a breeze that stirs the trees,
We find solace, pure and free.
Hand in hand, no need for words,
In this realm, love's spirit soars.

Underneath the starry sky,
Softly let our spirits fly.
In this dance, our souls align,
Bound by joy, so rare, divine.

Celestial Fancies in the Moon's Embrace

Beneath the moon, our dreams unite,
Celestial thoughts take gentle flight.
Veils of starlight kiss the sea,
Whispers echo, wild and free.

In a world that softly glows,
Magic lingers, love bestows.
Every twinkle tells a tale,
Guiding us on night's soft sail.

Echoes of a distant song,
In the night, we both belong.
Secrets held in shadows deep,
Celestial fancies, ours to keep.

When the dawn begins to break,
With the light, our hearts awake.
Yet in dreams, we'll still remain,
Bound by love, against the grain.

Whispers fade with morning's light,
But in hearts, we'll hold the night.
Celestial thoughts that drift and roam,
In the moon's embrace, we find home.

Upwards Giggles Touching the Heavens

In the garden where dreams sway,
Children laugh and dance and play.
Upwards giggles fill the air,
Finding joy everywhere.

Sunbeams paint the sky with cheer,
Echoes of their laughter near.
Tiny feet that skip and glide,
Hearts aglow, there's naught to hide.

Clouds above, like cotton candy,
Tickle toes that feel so dandy.
Every smile, a spark of light,
Touching heavens, pure delight.

In this place where worries cease,
Moments bloom and hearts find peace.
Laughter ringing, sweet and clear,
Upwards giggles shun all fear.

As the stars begin to shine,
Joyful hearts break every line.
Like the moon, our spirits rise,
Boundless dreams fill starlit skies.

Shimmering Refrains of the Evening

Evening falls, a soft embrace,
Whispers dance in twilight's grace.
Shimmering refrains fill the night,
Melodies that feel just right.

Moonlight spills on velvet ground,
In the silence, magic found.
Every sigh, a soothing balm,
In this hour, the world is calm.

Stars awaken, twinkling gold,
Gentle stories yet untold.
In the stillness, dreams take wing,
Echoes of the nightbirds sing.

Moments drift like fragrant air,
Whispers linger everywhere.
Shimmering dreams, our hearts entwined,
In this lull, true peace we find.

As the dawn begins to chase,
Evening's warmth we must embrace.
Yet the echoes shall remain,
In shimmering refrains, our gain.

The Universe's Playful Grin

Stars twinkle softly in the night,
Each a beacon, a gentle light.
Planets spin with joyful glee,
Whispers of cosmic irony.

Galaxies dance in endless space,
A swirling waltz, a bold embrace.
Comets dash with joyous cheer,
Painting trails, bright and clear.

Nebulas glow with colors bright,
A canvas drawn in the heart of night.
The universe chuckles, vast and grand,
A playful grin across the land.

From meteor showers to lunar beams,
Reality bends in whimsical dreams.
Echoes of laughter fill the air,
In the vast playground, free from care.

So gaze up high, let your heart soar,
For the universe plays forevermore.
In every spark, in every twirl,
Lives a playful grin that brightens the world.

Glistening Smiles Through the Gloom

Clouds may gather, shadows creep,
Yet through the darkness, glimmers leap.
Raindrops dance upon the ground,
In their rhythm, joy is found.

Sullen skies hold fast their weight,
But in each tear, there's hidden fate.
A smile glistens through the gray,
Shining hope will find a way.

When storms rage fierce and tempests howl,
Nature's beauty wears a scowl.
Yet life persists, with laughter's grace,
A glowing warmth in the darkest place.

Amidst the gloom, a spark ignites,
A reminder of colorful nights.
Splashes of joy in drizzles fall,
Glistening smiles break down the wall.

So hold on tight, let spirits rise,
For even gloom wears bright disguise.
In shadows deep, let laughter bloom,
Find the glistening smiles through the gloom.

Charm of Laughter Above the Canopy

Whispers of wind through rustling leaves,
Echo the laughter nature weaves.
Branches sway in a sunlit breeze,
Charmed by the joy of playful trees.

Beneath the boughs, the children play,
In secret worlds, where dreams stray.
Each giggle spills from hidden glens,
A melody that never ends.

The warmth of sun, the cool of shade,
In this realm, worries fade.
Flowers bloom with colors bright,
Their petals dance towards the light.

Above the canopy, laughter swells,
A harmony that nature tells.
In every rustle, in every sigh,
A reminder that joy will never die.

So join the song, let spirits soar,
In laughter's charm, forevermore.
Beneath the trees, let happiness begin,
In the embrace of laughter's spin.

Starlight Sparkles of Amusement

Glowing gems in the night sky,
Whispering secrets as they fly.
Each twinkle hides a playful jest,
Starlight sparkles, a cosmic fest.

In the vastness, dreams take flight,
A tapestry woven with pure delight.
Celestial tunes fill the air,
Comets brush past without a care.

Moonbeams tease with silvery grace,
Lighting up the darkened space.
Winking stars, in playful beams,
Invite us all to chase our dreams.

In the stillness, laughter rings,
As the universe spins, it sings.
Each heartbeat echoes a joy profound,
In starlight sparkles, we are found.

So lift your eyes, let joy abide,
In the cosmic dance, let your heart glide.
For in every twinkle, there's a story spun,
Starlight sparkles, our laughter's begun.

Moonlit Mischief in the Cosmos

In the quiet of the night,
Whispers of the stars take flight.
Giggling planets dance with glee,
While comets drift so wild and free.

Lunar laughter fills the air,
Tickling dreams beyond compare.
Shooting stars play hide and seek,
As secrets stir in shadows sleek.

Galaxies twirl with playful grace,
Cascading light through endless space.
Nebulae burst in vibrant hues,
As cosmic tunes weave through the blues.

Asteroids roll, a merry band,
In harmonious, stardust land.
Moonbeams weave in silvery strands,
While quiet wonders fill our hands.

Join the dance of night so bright,
In moonlit mischief, pure delight.
Together lost, yet found anew,
In cosmic tales our hearts pursue.

Celestial Joys in an Alluring Night

Stars like diamonds shining bold,
Whispers of the night unfold.
Planets twirl in joyful bliss,
In the cosmos' gentle kiss.

Galaxies swirl, a waltz divine,
Comets trace a silvery line.
Dreams are born in the night's embrace,
With every twinkle, a warm trace.

Moonbeams dance upon the sea,
Painting tales of you and me.
Each heartbeat syncs with cosmic play,
As time melts softly, night to day.

Ethereal visions fill the skies,
With every blink, a new surprise.
The universe hums a sweet refrain,
As we lose ourselves in joy's domain.

On this night, let worries cease,
In celestial joys, we find peace.
With stardust brushed upon our lips,
We float on dreams, on moonbeam ships.

Ethereal Joyride Through the Stars

Strap in tight, the journey starts,
With vibrant lights that warm our hearts.
Shooting stars, our speedway bright,
Dancing through the velvet night.

Galactic highways stretch so wide,
As cosmic wonders become our guide.
Whirling nebulae, a painted show,
In this grand ride where magic flows.

Celestial bodies twirl and glide,
On waves of stardust, we take the ride.
Life's troubles fade, a distant hum,
In this laughter, our spirits drum.

From one bright world to another we soar,
With each new view, we crave for more.
The universe cradles us in light,
On this joyful, wondrous flight.

Every moment, a treasure found,
In the boundless skies, we're glory-bound.
With each adventure, let our souls sing,
In an ethereal joyride, the cosmos brings.

Lighthearted Tales from the Midnight Sky

Underneath the silver glow,
Countless stories start to flow.
Stars sketch tales in twinkling light,
As dreams unfold, the world feels right.

Softly sung, the nightbird's song,
A melody where we belong.
Every shimmer, a whispered cheer,
In the solitude, love draws near.

Nebulas wink, sharing their lore,
As laughter echoes, forever more.
Planets spin, a merry chase,
Embraced by love in every space.

Jovial stars form endless rings,
Inviting everyone to sing.
With every glance, a spark ignites,
In lighthearted tales, our hearts take flight.

Through cosmic dance, the world we share,
Hand in hand, without a care.
Underneath the midnight sky,
We gather tales as laughter flies.

Gleeful Reflections on Midnight's Canvas

In shadows deep, the laughter plays,
Bright stars twinkle in playful ways.
Each whisper brings a joy unbound,
As midnight's canvas spins around.

Colors dance in dreamlike swirls,
Moonlight graces all the worlds.
Hearts alight with dreams to share,
In this moment, without a care.

Softly sighs the evening breeze,
Carrying hopes like floating leaves.
Every glance, a spark ignites,
Guiding us through gentle nights.

Reflections shimmer, joys unfold,
In silver hues, stories told.
Gleeful echoes fill the air,
A treasure found, beyond compare.

As dawn's first light begins to creep,
We hold these memories so deep.
In hearts we cherish, they will stay,
A gleeful dance that won't decay.

Jests and Sparks in Heaven's Theater

Curtains rise on a starry stage,
The universe bursts forth with mirth and rage.
Celestial jesters dance and spin,
As echoes of laughter swirl from within.

Galaxies twinkle with playful grace,
Each star a smile, a cheerful face.
Jests play out in cosmic might,
Under the glow of the velvet night.

Planets swirl in a joyful song,
In this theater, we all belong.
Sprightly comets dash and sway,
Chasing laughter, guiding our way.

With sparks of light that blaze and gleam,
Each moment feels like a dream.
In heaven's play, the heart takes flight,
A wondrous journey through the night.

So gather close, enjoy the show,
As the cosmos whispers low.
With every jest, our spirits rise,
In laughter, we find our skies.

Twinkling Grins in the Cosmic Sea

Beneath the stretch of the night so wide,
Twinkling grins in starlight glide.
Rippling waves of a galaxy bright,
Guide us softly into the night.

In the cosmic sea, we laugh and twirl,
Every twinkle a radiant pearl.
Hearts entwined in the starlit gleam,
Floating softly on love's sweet dream.

Celestial tides embrace our souls,
Filling our hearts with countless goals.
The universe hums a gentle tune,
While we dance beneath a silver moon.

Every star a wish we send,
To the infinite, our dreams extend.
In sparkling waters, we now sail,
On joyous currents, we prevail.

So hold this moment, pure and dear,
In the cosmic sea, we have no fear.
With twinkling grins lighting the way,
We journey on, come what may.

Glee Unfurled on Starlit Wings

With starlit wings, we rise and soar,
Across the skies, forevermore.
In laughter's embrace, our spirits sing,
A tapestry woven of joy we bring.

Galactic breezes whisper sweet,
As we twirl high, our hearts a beat.
In the velvet night, our dreams take flight,
On glee's bright path, we chase the light.

The cosmos blooms with colors anew,
With every moment, our joy rings true.
With open hearts, we ride the breeze,
In a dance of wonders, we find our ease.

Each star a spark, igniting delight,
Guiding us through this endless night.
With glee unfurled, in unity we chase,
The magic found in this sacred space.

So let us fly, unbound and free,
In the realm of bliss, just you and me.
With starlit wings of joy, we sing,
Embraced by the wonders that life can bring.

Mirage of Cheer in the Midnight Wash

In the still night air, dreams softly sway,
Whispers of laughter, floating away.
Colors of joy in shadows they weave,
A fleeting moment, hard to believe.

Rippling echoes dance through the gloom,
Painting the dark with a vibrant bloom.
Each heartbeat echoes, a soft serenade,
In the twilight's embrace, fears start to fade.

Stars overhead twinkle, secrets they keep,
Crafting a tapestry, vibrant and deep.
In the mirage, where hopes intertwine,
Midnight's magic, a life so divine.

Moonbeams whisper, secrets of night,
Transforming shadows into pure light.
Here we find laughter, a luminous spark,
Chasing the dark, igniting the arc.

Moments suspended, as if to enthrall,
Each note of joy, like a soft, sweet call.
Through the midnight wash, colors emerge,
Cheer in the silence, a blissful surge.

Dance of Delight in Shadowed Light

In the pattern of dusk, where shadows reside,
A dance of delight, with grace as our guide.
Steps intertwine in a rhythmic embrace,
Under the veil of the night's gentle face.

Whirling in laughter, we spin through the dark,
Each twirl releasing a shimmering spark.
With whispers of glee, we glide and we sway,
In this sweet ballet, we chase fears away.

Hidden in corners, soft silences throng,
Echoes of joy in a silvery song.
Each glimmering star joins in the fun,
Casting soft shadows as the dance is spun.

Fading away, the worries we meet,
In this serenade, our hearts find their beat.
Under the veil, we both come alive,
As the rhythm of joy forever shall thrive.

Through the landscape of night, we dance as one,
Chasing the shadows until the night's done.
In this moment's grace, we rise and we fall,
A dance of delight, embracing it all.

The Universe's Lighthearted Waltz

Beneath the vast sky, the cosmos conspires,
To weave a waltz that lifts us higher.
Galaxies swirling in a joyful embrace,
Each twinkling star a smile on its face.

Gravity's pull, a gentle caress,
Launching our hearts into boundless finesse.
With every heartbeat, the planets align,
In this lighthearted dance, you are mine.

Across the expanse, where dreams take flight,
The universe beckons, igniting the night.
In the soft glimmer of stardust we trust,
For each shared moment, a treasure must lust.

As comets flash by in luminous trails,
We sway with the rhythm as silence unveils.
In the vastness around, our spirits abide,
The lighthearted waltz, forever our guide.

In this cosmic ballet, we twirl and we spin,
Lost in the magic of where we begin.
With each gentle whisper, the cosmos sings,
A celestial dance, where love takes its wings.

So let us encompass the universe wide,
In this lighthearted waltz, you're here by my side.
Together we'll dance through the realms of the night,
As the stars above us forever shine bright.

Star-Kissed Banter in the Air

In the cradle of night, a soft banter flows,
As stars twinkle bright, and moonlight glows.
Words in the silence, a delicate trace,
A symphony whispered, a warm embrace.

Floating like feathers, light as the air,
Laughter a melody, weaving a care.
With every exchange, the cosmos will cheer,
Our star-kissed banter, drawing us near.

Clouds drift above, a canvas of dreams,
Painting our thoughts in silvery streams.
In moments of stillness, we find our delight,
Under the blanket of the softest night.

With playful glances and smiles intertwined,
The universe listens, our hearts unconfined.
Each word a note in a celestial song,
A star-kissed serenade where we belong.

In the embrace of the night, laughter ascends,
A laughter that echoes, as time gently bends.
With every breath shared, authenticity thrived,
In this star-kissed banter, we joyfully strive.

As dawn draws near, the magic won't fade,
In memories crafted, our hearts have been made.
So let's cherish the moments, light as the air,
For in star-kissed banter, our love is laid bare.

Delightful Echoes from the Cosmic Depths

Whispers of stars dance in the night,
Singing softly, a cosmic flight.
Galaxies twirl in a vibrant hue,
Echoes of joy, old yet new.

Planets spin in a graceful waltz,
A tapestry where time exalts.
Meteor trails like fleeting dreams,
In the void, joy's laughter beams.

Nebulae sigh with colors bright,
Veils of wonder take their flight.
Celestial bodies in harmony sway,
Binding darkness in a playful way.

Stellar wind carries stories untold,
In the silence, mysteries unfold.
Every twinkle, a hymn of night,
Casting shadows, bathing in light.

In cosmic depths, where silence reigns,
Delightful echoes break all chains.
Reveling in the universe's song,
In this dance, we all belong.

Twilight Giggles Across the Firmament

As day meets night, the sky blushes,
Whispers of laughter in the hushes.
Stars popping out like pearls on lace,
Twilight giggles, a gentle grace.

Clouds drift by in whimsical forms,
Softening shadows through evening storms.
Fireflies flicker their tiny lights,
Creating magic on summer nights.

The moon plays peekaboo, oh so bright,
Winking down with delight in sight.
Galaxies wink, a silent jest,
In this twilight, they do their best.

Echoes of joy weave through the air,
Twilight whispers adventures to share.
Beneath the arch of wondrous skies,
Dreams take flight like birds that rise.

In this realm of evening serenade,
Laughter dances, never to fade.
Hearts align with shadows that play,
In the twilight, we find our way.

Enigmatic Smiles in the Celestial Realm

Stars wear a smile, a radiant glow,
In the vastness where secrets flow.
Comets brush past with a knowing grin,
In the celestial dance, life begins.

Constellations weave tales of yore,
Enigmatic whispers invite us to explore.
Waves of stardust, a sparkling embrace,
In the cosmos, we find our place.

Nebulae cradle wisps of delight,
Painting the canvas of the infinite night.
With every pulse, the universe sighs,
Enigmatic smiles shine through the skies.

As moons align, hope flickers anew,
Lighting paths where dreams come true.
Infinity holds secrets vast and deep,
In the celestial realm, wonders leap.

Echoes of laughter ripple through space,
In the starlit domain, we carve our trace.
Where enigmas whisper and wonders embrace,
In this tapestry, we find our grace.

Joyful Horizons Beneath the Stars

Dancing in twilight, spirits take flight,
Horizons bloom with colors so bright.
Each star a wish, shimmering high,
A canvas of dreams painted in the sky.

Under the veil of the sparkling night,
Laughter and love ignite the light.
Constellations twinkling with glee,
A joyful horizon, wild and free.

The moon, a sentinel, watches in grace,
Guiding hearts to a sacred space.
In the stillness, our hopes entwine,
Finding beauty in the divine.

Fireworks of starlight burst and play,
As night unfolds, it lights the way.
Every heartbeat a cosmic melody,
In this universe, we're truly free.

With every dawn, new horizons call,
Echoes of joy, embracing us all.
Beneath the stars, our spirits soar,
In this journey, forever explore.

Whispers of Joy Beneath the Stars

In the hush of night we find,
Soft whispers dancing in our mind.
Stars twinkle like laughter bright,
Each sparkle a promise of delight.

Dreams take flight on gentle breeze,
Carried high through ancient trees.
Joy ripples through the cosmic sea,
In this vast expanse, we are free.

Moonlight drapes a silver shroud,
Casting shadows, serene and proud.
Underneath this sky, we sing,
A melody of love's sweet spring.

A symphony of distant lands,
Where hope and harmony expand.
Tender hearts are intertwined,
In the universe, peace we find.

With each twinkling star above,
We gather strength, we spread our love.
Together, we shine in the dark,
In a journey, we leave a mark.

Serenade of Gleaming Giggles

In the glade where laughter flows,
Tiny giggles burst and glow.
Fairies dance in the moonlight's grace,
Spreading joy in this enchanted space.

With every tickle, every tease,
The forest echoes in playful frees.
Whispers swirl like leaves in flight,
Gleaming giggles paint the night.

Underneath the glowing trees,
Magic hums upon the breeze.
Dreamers gather, faces aglow,
Sharing secrets only they know.

Stars nod along to soft refrain,
As laughter lifts us once again.
Echoes bounce in tender waves,
In hearts, the joy of youth saves.

Time surrenders, moments blend,
Every giggle a magic send.
In this serenade we reside,
Where laughter is our faithful guide.

Celestial Chuckles Above

Up above, the night sky beams,
Celestial chuckles weave our dreams.
Stars giggle in their playful glow,
Lighting paths where wishes go.

Moonbeams twirl and spin with glee,
Painting stories for you and me.
Across the void, laughter rings,
In harmony with cosmic things.

Each twinkling star, a jester bright,
Sprinkling joy through the velvet night.
With every wink, they sprinkle cheer,
Whispers of love we hold so near.

Together, we gaze, lost in thought,
Sharing laughter that time forgot.
In this moment, all is right,
Celestial chuckles shining bright.

Forever bound by the sky's embrace,
In the cosmos, we find our place.
United by laughter, strong and true,
The universe smiles with me and you.

Radiant Echoes in the Twilight

As daylight fades to twilight's hue,
Radiant echoes call to you.
Soft whispers brush the evening air,
Starlit secrets begin to share.

Colors blend in a gentle sigh,
Painting dreams against the sky.
Echoes shimmer in dusk's embrace,
Awakening magic, a tranquil pace.

In this moment, still and bright,
Joy dances in the fading light.
Every heartbeat, every glow,
Fills the night with love's soft flow.

Fleeting shadows, tender grace,
In twilight's lap, we find our place.
Harmonies of the heart unite,
Radiant echoes hold us tight.

Together, we dream beneath the sky,
In the twilight, love will not die.
With every star, our spirits rise,
Beneath the canvas of endless skies.

Moonlit Mirth and Cosmic Play

In silver beams the shadows play,
Whispers of night lead dreams astray,
Stars twinkle in a graceful sway,
While moonlit mirth invites to stay.

The world beneath a cosmic dome,
Soft beams guide us away from home,
With every laugh, we feel the roam,
As joy gathers in its vast poem.

Laughter dances like fireflies,
Illuminating the darkened skies,
In this celestial disguise,
We find the truth that never lies.

Hearts unite in the moon's embrace,
Finding comfort in silent grace,
Every moment we joyfully chase,
In this magical, shared space.

Beyond the night, the dawn will creep,
Yet memories of joy we keep,
As moonlit mirth begins to sleep,
In dreams where laughter softly sweeps.

Stars Dance with Delight

In twilight's hush, the stars ignite,
A tapestry of pure delight,
They waltz with grace, a lovely sight,
Guided by the whispers of night.

Each twinkle tells a tale untold,
Of love and dreams, of hearts so bold,
In cosmic rhythms, bright and gold,
Their beauty makes the dark unfold.

As we gaze upward, spirits soar,
In the vastness, we seek for more,
With every shimmer, our hopes restore,
Each gentle pulse, a love encore.

With laughter's echo, hearts entwine,
Moonbeams glisten where we align,
In this dance, our souls define,
Together, under stars, we shine.

A night like this can never fade,
With memories in moments made,
Stars dance on, never afraid,
In the lure of night's cascade.

The Brightness of Joyful Whispers

In the stillness, whispers weave,
Tales of joy, of hearts that believe,
Softly spoken, they never deceive,
In every breath, the light we achieve.

A melody of laughter flows,
Where every kindness gently grows,
In cheerful notes, delight bestows,
The brightness in our hearts that glows.

With every sunrise, hope takes flight,
Painting the world, golden and bright,
In joyful whispers, pure delight,
Guides us through the day and night.

Together we'll play in vibrant hue,
Creating dreams and moments true,
In whispers of joy, we are renewed,
Finding magic in all we do.

So let us cherish every sound,
In joyous whispers, love is found,
For in this bond, we are unbound,
Together in brightness, forever crowned.

A Symphony of Smiles in the Dark

In shadows deep, our laughter rings,
A symphony that softly sings,
With every note, pure joy it brings,
Together we find what evening flings.

Smiles illuminate our weary way,
Guiding us through the night and sway,
In every glance, the stars display,
A dance of hearts where love will play.

With gentle whispers, secrets shared,
In every moment, love is declared,
Through radiant smiles, we are prepared,
To face the dark and not be scared.

Together we'll weave our dreams anew,
In a tapestry of me and you,
Under the night, our spirits flew,
Creating magic, a love so true.

So let this night be one to keep,
Where smiles shine bright and laughter leaps,
In this symphony, our hearts will seep,
In the dark, our promise deep.

www.ingramcontent.com/pod-product-compliance
Ingram Content Group UK Ltd.
Pitfield, Milton Keynes, MK11 3LW, UK
UKHW022126231224
452783UK00011B/433